D1068598

Béisbol! Latino Heroes of Major League Baseball

ALBERT PUJOLS

JOSH LEVENTHAL

WORLD BOOK

BOLT

This World Book edition of *Albert Pujols*
is published by agreement between
Black Rabbit Books and World Book, Inc.
© 2017 Black Rabbit Books,
2140 Howard Dr. West,
North Mankato, MN 56003 U.S.A.
World Book, Inc.,
180 North LaSalle St., Suite 900,
Chicago, IL 60601 U.S.A.

Design and Production by Michael Sellner
Photo Research by Rhonda Milbrett

Library of Congress Control Number: 2015954869

HC ISBN: 978-0-7166-9596-7   PB ISBN: 978-0-7166-9597-4

Printed in the United States at CG Book Printers,
North Mankato, Minnesota, 56003. PO #1797 4/16

*921 PUJ

Contents

CHAPTER 1

A Latino Legend

Albert Pujols steps up to the plate. It's the first **inning**, and there is no score. Pujols sends the ball deep to left field. Home run! That's number 499 in his **career**.

Four innings later, Pujols is up again. He smashes the ball into the seats. That makes 500 career home runs!

An All-Star Player

Pujols is a powerful baseball player. He is known for his great batting skills. He has hit more than 550 home runs so far in his career.

But Pujols wasn't always a pro ball player. He grew up in the Dominican Republic. His father often drank too much alcohol. Pujols had to help take care of him. Young Pujols had to make his own baseball equipment. Sometimes he used fruit for balls. He turned a milk carton into a glove.

Haiti

Dominican Republic

Number of Latino Major League Baseball Players

through 2015

642	Dominican Republic
341	Venezuela
253	Puerto Rico
193	Cuba
118	Mexico
55	Panama
17	Colombia
14	Curacao
14	Nicaragua
12	U.S. Virgin Islands
6	Bahamas
5	Aruba
4	Jamaica
3	Brazil
1	Belize
1	Honduras

CHAPTER 2

A Young Baseball Star

Pujols was born January 16, 1980. As a child, Pujols could hit a ball far. He was very fast too.

Pujols and his family moved to the United States in 1996. They hoped for a better life there. Sixteen-year-old Pujols could only speak Spanish. He studied hard to learn English in high school.

Playing in School

Pujols also worked hard at baseball. He made his high school team as the **shortstop**. He hit long home runs. He was named to the all-state team.

After high school, Pujols played for a community college. He hit a **grand slam** in his first college game.

Pujols went to high school in Independence, Missouri.

Drafted

Major league **scouts** watched Pujols play in college. Some scouts thought he wasn't a good enough fielder. But he sure could hit! The Cardinals picked Pujols in the 13th round of the 1999 **draft**.

Pujols played only one year in the minor leagues. His incredible batting proved he was ready for the majors.

Fun Facts

right handed

WEIGHT

230 POUNDS
(104 kilograms)

6 feet
3 inches
(1.9 m) tall

Pujols and his wife run a charity called the Pujols Family Foundation. It helps people with **Down syndrome.**

has many nicknames, including **"Prince Albert"** and **"The Machine"**

CHAPTER 3

In the

Majors

Pujols played with the Cardinals in 2001. He had a great season. He batted .329 with 37 home runs. He was chosen for the All-Star Team. After the season, Pujols was named National League **Rookie** of the Year.

A batting average shows how often a player gets a hit. An average of .300 is excellent.

Most Career Home Runs by Dominican-Born Players
(through 2015 season)

Vladimir Guerrero (1996–2011)
449

David Ortiz (1997–2015)
503

Most Valuable Player

Pujols kept getting better. In 2003, he led the league in hits, doubles, and runs. Pujols won the National League Most Valuable Player (MVP) award in 2005. He won MVP again in 2008 and 2009.

Pujols had at least 30 homers and a .300 average in 10 straight years. No other player has ever done that.

Manny Ramirez (1993–2011)	Albert Pujols (2001–2015)	Sammy Sosa (1989–2007)
555	560	**609**

World Series Champion

In 2004, Pujols' 46 home runs helped the Cardinals reach the World Series. They lost to the Red Sox. In 2006, Pujols and the Cardinals won the World Series. They won again in 2011. Pujols hit three homers in the 2011 series against the Rangers.

2004 World Series

Cardinals vs. Red Sox
games won: 0–4

Eye on the

2006
World
Series

Cardinals vs. Tigers
games won: 4-1

2011
World
Series

Cardinals vs. Rangers
games won: 4-3

CHAPTER 4

Continuing to

After the 2011 season, Pujols joined the Angels. He became a leader on the team right away. In 2015, he was named to his 10th All-Star Team. At age 35, he hit 40 home runs.

Pujols' Yearly MLB Batting Averages

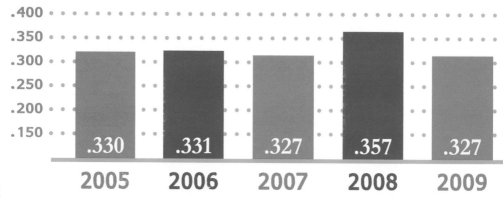

	2005	2006	2007	2008	2009
	.330	.331	.327	.357	.327

.312	.299	.285	.258	.272		.244
2010	2011	2012	2013	2014	2015

Runs ⌂ = 10 runs

Year	Runs
2005	129
2006	119
2007	99
2008	100
2009	124
2010	115
2011	105
2012	85
2013	49
2014	89
2015	85

Hits

195	177	185	187	186
2005	2006	2007	2008	2009

Games Played

2005	**161**	2008	**148**	2011	**147**	2014	**159**
2006	**143**	2009	**160**	2012	**154**	2015	**157**
2007	**158**	2010	**159**	2013	**99**		

Home Runs

41	49	32	37	47
2005	2006	2007	2008	2009

42	37	30	17	28	40
2010	2011	2012	2013	2014	2015

Runs Batted In

2005	2006	2007	2008	2009	2010	2011	2012	2013	2014	2015
117	137	103	116	135	118	99	105	64	105	95

183	173	173	101	172	147
2010	2011	2012	2013	2014	2015

Powerful Player

Pujols is one of the best hitters in baseball today. Fans love him. And his teammates do too. Many people think one day he'll be in the Baseball Hall of Fame.

Pujols' Awards (through 2015)

3 MVPs

6 ALL-STAR GAMES

2 GOLD GLOVES

Timeline

1980

January
Pujols is born.

1996
moves to Missouri

1999

August
joins the Cardinals

2001

April
plays first major league game

hits first major league home run

28

2006

October

Cardinals win the World Series

2011

October

Cardinals win the World Series

December

joins the Angels

2014

April

hits 500th home run

GLOSSARY

career (kuh-REER)—a period of time spent in a job

Down syndrome (DOWN SIN-drohm)—a condition someone is born with that causes mental and physical problems

draft (DRAFT)—a system in which new players are chosen for professional teams

grand slam (GRAND SLAM)—a home run with players on every base

inning (IN-ing)—one of the nine parts of a baseball game in which each team bats until three outs are made

Latino (luh-TEE-no)—from Mexico or a country in South America, Central America, or the Caribbean

rookie (ROOK-ee)—a first-year player

scout (SKOWT)—a person sent to get information about someone or something

shortstop (SHORT-stop)—the player who defends the area between second and third base

BOOKS

Frisch, Aaron. *Albert Pujols*. The Big Time. Mankato, MN: Creative Education, 2013.

Herman, Gail. *What Is the World Series?* What Was …? New York: Grosset & Dunlap, 2015.

Young, Jeff C. *Albert Pujols: A Baseball Star Who Cares*. Sports Stars Who Care. Berkeley Heights, NJ: Enslow Publishers, 2014.

WEBSITES

Albert Pujols
m.mlb.com/player/405395/albert-pujols

Baseball
www.ducksters.com/sports/baseball.php

Official Los Angeles Angels Website
losangeles.angels.mlb.com

INDEX